Initial Meeting

N.M. Sanchez

In thought, in passing, in the brushing of hands. I hope you find something to take with you, to keep close. I hope you enjoy our *initial meeting.*

CONTENTS

ACKNOWLEDGMENTS

A thank you to my family, for the roots that
flourished to give me life.

01. THE FEELING IS REAL

The crushing reality that your fantasies are confined to day dreams.

There is a war inside you begging for peace. I pray you find your strength.

There was a confusion that came with being taught to give freely, to give without expecting anything in return when so many others only knew how to take and take and take until they left you empty.

I wonder how many of us are still waiting for an apology we'll never receive.

You will never love another the same way, again.
And I'm still trying to figure out if that's a
blessing or a tragedy.

I had offered myself to you – bare and selfless,
with nothing but good intentions
and a seemingly false hope that you would
reciprocate it.

How often has the timing been wrong? How often have we had to move along like we didn't feel something?

One minute they ache to touch you, the next day they want nothing to do with you. Feelings are a fickle thing. You want answers, you need closure, and now you're laying awake at night trying to hold yourself together because you allowed yourself to be vulnerable. You are full of love for someone who saw what you had to offer – and they decided they didn't want it. This, an unbearable version of the many forms of loneliness.

I have bended back and over for a man
who's only intention was to watch me break.
Imagine his surprise when I rose from the dirt
he left me in.

I had offered myself long enough – my thoughts, my soul, my body. I had provided him with a form of unconditional love that he otherwise only felt at the hands of his mother. But I must have done something wrong, held by filthy hands for far too long, I blamed myself. I settled.

Wars have been declared over miscommunication, but you wonder what destroyed us.

Sex for the sake of it – nothing more than my body responding out of habit. What a waste, what a bore, what a crime when your heart is not invested.

That's the way it goes.

One day, he leaves you for another woman. And one day, you are "the other woman."

I've left him intrigued – he proposes an idea via
text message moments after I had gone my way:

"I wonder how many men have envisioned
an entire life with you upon the initial meeting."

I came full of questions and curiosity – not an illusion of who I think you are.

It's pathetic, isn't it? To sit here and believe that there is some sort of otherworldly love out there that I have yet to experience? And believing in its possibility, hoping that there is more out there than whatever it is I have already felt, because there has to be more? Because I refuse to believe that this is all there is.

You can share similar interests
and still not have chemistry.

Maybe it's wrong of me to feel this way,
but that doesn't make it any less real.

There is power in seduction, on bringing a man to his knees. Turned on – I get off by feeding into his fantasies.

I'm your girl, I say. *Now how do you want me?*

This is not a poem – but a cry. I have so many questions and you've gone silent.

Rekindle an old flame
get burned, again.

It's an unbearable truth. At different times in my life, I have been on either side of the coin:

Wondering how often you looked at me, wishing I was her / and wondering how often you looked at her, wishing she was me.

You are here, you are there
your heart is often elsewhere.

I wonder who she is,
I wonder who I am to you.

I loved you for all the reasons why you thought
you couldn't love yourself.

I don't know what I'm waiting for,
but I'm impatient.

I need to stop offering the warmth of my hands
to those who turn their cheeks and only offer the
cold shoulder.

Either nothing would come of it or I'd ache to touch you. I'll never tell you, but it was the latter.

It was one of two things: either you'd kiss me now or forever regret that you didn't.

The reality of me
was not nearly as enticing
as the idea of me,
I know that now.

You craved me once, I now ache for the past.

When the wound has almost healed –
someone will pass by to dig in their fingers.

You say you want to, "try again." But I know it's never going to be the same. I know that this is just a desperate attempt to save years worth of our relationship. You say you want to, "try again." But I know that we're just buying time. We're putting a band-aid on a laceration knowing damn well we won't survive this.

We sit together and I speak an awful lot to busy
ears that do not listen.
–
We lay together and I ache an awful lot because I
know he does not love me.

I wanted to kiss you goodbye. I wanted to make sure you knew what you were losing.

Listen – the older I get, the more I realize we're all just walking around in our own personal hell. This is how we've come to acknowledge the value of kindness. This is why we spend hours or days thinking about the kind act of a stranger when we felt the world was against us.

He broke my heart daily,
made a poet out of me.

You were a riddle I couldn't solve
a question I couldn't answer
and I would love to spend forever
figuring you out.

Please don't do it, don't you wait by the phone. Because here you are, waiting, and he's kissing her goodnight.

"I love you's" on our tongue
we leave our hearts with each other
but walk in different directions.

I've been trying to piece it together – when did you stop loving me and was it my fault? I've drowned in self-blame looking for answers.

Being "naked" had nothing to do
with my skirt falling at your feet
or my bra at the edge of your bed
instead
it was then when - without question
I cried and you held me.

If only people were more honest with each other
– now imagine the poetry in that.

You're right – love and trust
go hand in hand
but both my hands are empty.

For how many times I have been here – and it
still hurts all the same.

We're either falling in love or falling apart or meeting somewhere in the middle, and the middle is a state of complacency I am much too restless to settle for.

I ache in places where only his hands can reach.

But I am merely a flower,
begging for his light.

Despite all of your mistakes,
I stayed – and that was mine.

I hope you find someone
who holds you
like you're the greatest piece of art
God's ever put in their hands.

You held me as I cried
and I had been here before
in the arms of a man who
was awfully good at
pretending to love me.

You told me that you loved me
from my head to my toes
but I have broken my own bones
trying to find
where you put this so-called love.

I often reach out
in the middle of the night
for the warmth of your back
for a hand that's not there.

When will I see you, again?

I loved you through your darkest times,
but you ran when I spoke of my troubles.

Please, please, please
do not throw yourself
in to the arms of another
in attempt to forget,
the one that once held you.

Hold yourself together.

I have fallen apart
to watch you come together.

How many times does he have to let you down before you realize you're the only one who's going to pick yourself up?

Would you have held me tighter if you knew it'd be the last time?

You have to go through the storm if you want to see the sun.

Women will either admire your confidence – or despise you for it.

You taste like something my mother would of told me to spit out because it was, "no good."

Don't depend on another man
to heal the wounds another made
when he pressed his lips against your skin
and left unexpectedly.

Who am I kidding?
Goodbye is much too big of a mouthful
when all I've dreamt about
are your hello's.

Somewhere between the stillness of it all, with
his hand at my neck and our lips barely touching.
I thought, my god. If only it was you.

And when you find me
I hope that your heart pounds
and your mouth waters
and your eyes glisten.
I hope the hunger grows,
I hope you ache to touch me.

I have the awful habit
of pouring my heart out
and in to people
who have no room for me.

Sometimes you lose a love
sometimes you lose a friend
but in truth, you lose both
every time, either way.

I've learned that home is where the heart is and I left it with you.

I am drained. Spent. Sinking in to this bed after a long day of having to explain why we no longer belong to each other.

You were the kind of love
that made sense on paper
but not in his heart.

It was a defense mechanism, wasn't it? Ignoring me until I went away? Because I offered kindness and you did not know what to do with it.

You have loved too much and have not been
loved enough.

Searching for love within myself before I look for it in you.

You couldn't let go of the past
so I left you in mine.

It's something you know almost instantly, how important someone is going to be to you, whether or not the sun will rise and the moon will set with them.

You left – and it felt like I was already surviving the worst thing that could ever happen to me.

Here's the thing, I don't want to dream anymore. Come to me – run. Kiss me like I hold the answer to your existence. Reignite the passion lying dormant within my ribcage.

I rushed to love you, falling at your feet, giving you the responsibility to fix me – letting you press your lips against my wounds as a substitute for band-aids. It is no one's fault but my own. This is not an apology.

I drowned in the promise of our future, the one you planted at the base of my heart that started to grow around me like vines on a house - only to have your earthquakes tear it down. This is not an apology.

I dreamt in your native tongue, caliente y apasionado, you asked me to let you in - y no queria vivir sin ti. But it's no secret, I always want what isn't good for me. This is not an apology.

You tasted like the truth past lovers failed to give me. They were not as good at their word play. You told me I was poetry. But this is not the first time dirty hands have held me. This is not an apology.

I loved you, whole heartedly, passionately, undoubtedly. It would be a waste of energy to regret it. You have been the first. I hope you treasure it. This is not an apology.

I Have Loved You, I Am Not Sorry

It's just one of those things, you know? You go on for weeks and weeks at a time and you're fine, you still think about him but you're fine. Then comes that one dreadful morning where you're walking down the stairs half-asleep and into the kitchen and you pour yourself a cup of coffee and cry because you remembered. You wash the dishes and cry because you remembered. You treat yourself to a pint of your favorite ice cream and cry into it because you remembered – and the world doesn't let you forget him.

If I could find the tiniest speck of goodness in others, I hold on to it no matter how poorly they treat me. I stick around like a dog who's been kicked and doesn't know how to go due to the sense of loyalty that sits behind my rib cage.

It's almost as if I have to offer my body in exchange for a listener. Conversations lacking depth, connections are fickle. Genuine care and understanding, where do I find it and does it exist with my clothes on? Because the pretty girl tells you what keeps her up at night and you realize it isn't really what you're here for.

We're in the backseat of your car and my fingers are tracing over the lines of your palm and you ask me what my favorite song is. I tell you and you ask to hear it. I could feel my heart beating out of my chest as if I had just dropped the curtain, feeling vulnerable without truly understanding why.

I tell you that it's soft and slow and that I can't really explain why it means so much to me, just that it does. Kind of like the way I was drawn to you before we even met, feeling as if I had to know you, how I ached to know you. How I fell in tune to your frequency without truly understanding why.

I look down, you're holding my hand.

When I was younger I remember being told things like, "Don't show too much skin, make him wonder. Don't tell him how you feel, keep him guessing. Guys don't like it when you talk about your feelings, you're going to scare him away. You're coming on too strong. Don't show too much interest. Let him chase you. Let him text you first because you don't want to seem too eager."

However, nothing feels better than being so unapologetically you. If someone isn't feeling you, that's okay. Nothing would have blossomed with that person, anyway. There are so many people in this world, someone's going to catch a glimpse of your light. And the best part is - they're going to want to step in it, without fear, for wanting to explore all that you are.

It's like the sun hasn't come up since you left.

There's so much I want to do, so many things I've yet to experience. I'm a bundle of softness and love and I want to share it. But so often I find myself having to wait. Waiting for the right time, if there ever was, is, or will be. I'm running a hundred miles an hour but stuck in place and it's exhausting.

You ever love someone so much you wish things were as simple as kissing their pain away? Because "sorry" doesn't quite cut it and "give it time" is just too intangible and all you can do is sit there with them, in silence, wishing that holding their hand was enough.

I will be fixed before I love you. Stitched back together by my own hands. I will become the best version of myself – for myself, and then for you. These hands, they're small, but they'll carry the world for you if that's what you wanted. And I will love you with a heavy heart despite how many times it's been broken.

02. SPLIT THEORY

The trouble is, you think there's only one reality.

I entertain the multiverse theory considerably. To think multiple versions of ourselves inhabit a variety of parallel universes. To think that we exist – not in two places at once – but beyond, infinitely. I wonder about myself or rather, I wonder about *her*. What her days look like, who she is with, her taste in music, food, if she is still "here" wherever that may be, if she is doing alright for herself.

I could not understand what I felt,
only that it was there.

Maybe you loved me, Maybe you love me, Maybe you will.

What if this whole notion of "love at first sight" is not totally as bizarre as I once thought it to be? Within seconds upon meeting someone, we realize whether or not we are attracted to them, it's something that happens almost instantly. And to me, it's never been some sort of grand event where I've seen a man and believed him to be the one I was going to spend the rest of my life with - but I've seen a man and felt drawn to him beyond my understanding. So then I wondered about time and space and parallel universes and entertained this idea that maybe we already exist together in one. Maybe we're existing together somewhere and when I look at you with a heavy heart and familiarity, that is the connection we feel. This "love at first sight" may technically be a second one. This gut feeling is only the hinting of us having existed (or already existing together) somewhere in time. And maybe it's not love right away or at all but you can't deny that *click*.

And that *click* is a phenomenal event.

The softest encounter,
a twisted fantasy.

You compare her to the flowers,
I am convinced I'm all thorn.

He has two faces – one where he's in love with me and one where he pretends to be in love with you.

Words render useless, crash into me.

Tell me about your day dreams. How often have you made love to me?

Imagine that – your body
a vessel, a safe haven
to something much more
complex and ethereal.

Admire the rose, accept her thorns.

You often find me distracted, my body is present but my mind is elsewhere. You bring me back to the now – in question. "Why do you do that? Stare off into space?" but I assumed it was obvious. I assumed they knew us dreamers couldn't bare the thought of our reality.

A spell is brewing at my hips – dripping honey.
Men offer their tongues, but I prefer my solitude.

I wanted so desperately to know another soul who's hands were only eager to undress me. I conjured up ways to keep his interest, foolishly hoping he would find something worth staying for other than the magic of my thighs.

I molded myself to fit his concept of delicacy, of desire, of a mouth watering dream.

So much so, I lived as another woman – in attempts to maintain an illusion of some otherworldly passion. I wanted him to devour me whole even if it meant I must wear a mask.

There is adoration in the cosmos
and I am drowning in the abyss of possibilities
my heart has known you
long before I was ever conscious
of your existence
there is a force I once fought against
that now, I choose to flow with.

What if I've always known you?

I hope you don't have the pleasure of finding me in dreams when you're the one who chose to close the door on our reality.

I was a burning flame,
he was made of rain.

The mirror, a trickster, gifting deceit –
another world lives beyond the glass.

A lost opportunity, a day dream I keep slipping into. You are a mouthful of *what if's*.

You ever just look at somebody and it's like your soul aches to touch them?

I'm a temporary being consumed by a lifetime of fantasies.

I wish I wasn't such a dreamer. I've ruined this life for myself.

Everything felt as though the stars themselves arranged our meeting, as if the stars themselves bumped elbows and smiled – wishing upon us.

You are the epitome of
some otherworldly love.
I swear, I must have known you
in a past life.

It amazes me how certain people seem to fall into your life at the right time. You met them by chance or fate or what have you but it is only when they happen to you that you realize you actually needed them. It's like the universe said, "So and so can fix this" and sent them on their way to you.

I think about you at a distance like a stranger passing me by on the street. Like that guy sitting in a corner at the bookstore with his headphones in. That guy sitting two tables down from mine at the diner. We are worlds apart but I can feel it in my bones that somewhere, we are together.

Subjectivity is a fickle thing
often breeding illusion.
A varied reality among individuals.

I thought one look would reel you in
the way the moon pulls on the earth.
I thought I might cause a storm
I thought I might rattle your oceans.

What is the passing of time to an individual who cannot recall the memories to prove it?

There's a thrill that comes from a love that's forbidden, the way our shadows sneak a kiss when the others aren't looking.

I hope she tastes me in your mouth
feels me in your heart
and finds me in your laugh.

He wrote of me as if one had the ability
to contain beauty in a sentence.

I am sensual
emotional, mischievous
phenomenal
and I rattle him to his core.

He tosses my luscious curves
into the bodies of paragraphs –
thick and bolded.

He touches me
and I burn the tip of his fingers.

I made the mistake of taking you
to every place that I loved
'cause now I've got no where to run
without running into you.

I connected the dots while
you drew lines that ran parallel.
Nothing means anything
unless you believe it does.

You went on and on about a woman who smells of strawberries while I sat quietly in defeat. I thought vanilla was your favorite.

You're right – I wasn't thinking clearly. I needed you to kiss some sense into me.

In some parallel universe,
I know you held me tighter.
You tried harder.

You said, "Look my love, I will meet you
halfway."

But no one told me
this kind of sadness weighs heavy.
I sigh so deep, I sink into the earth.

A soft and sensual thrill, the fragility of heaven, an adventurous hell.

Lucid dreaming is a frightening yet exhilarating experience. To think, to act, to acknowledge that you are in fact within the dream world. To attain self-agency elsewhere while your body remains at home – in bed.

03. OF EXISTENCE

The opposite of death is not living
but mere existence. Existence is passive –
while to live is to be in search for meaning.

You will often find that at times you have to cut ties with the people you love, due to no fault of their own – but for the sake of self-preservation.

Reading, exploring, drowning in thought.
Trying to set my own soul on fire.

If people are their deepest thoughts and darkest secrets, I am convinced that no one really knows anybody.

Self-doubt and disappointment tend to stem from this false perception that someone else's success is your failure. It is a disservice to ourselves to remain in a constant competition with others - when we, as individuals, should only strive to better ourselves, our situations. You will achieve your goals quickly and more efficiently if you believe in your vision, and stay true to your version of it. Take your time, you'll get there. There is a way and you will find it.

I think it's the idea of being wanted that pulls you in and the affection that makes you stay, even when you don't feel a thing. Because we want to be wanted and we need to be loved and sometimes we're selfish, so we jump in even if the waters cold and steal the warmth of a man's love.

The longing, the conflict.

Indifference is the temporary death of a writer.

Embracing my femininity,
arms open to a spiritual growth
allowing for an authentic sense
of self.

It's an automatic thought, a gut instinct
– being somewhere, doing something with
someone and understanding that your
personality will not flourish here.

Dive into what exhilarates your being, despite the fear you may experience. To find what moves you and to flow with it is progress towards self-fulfillment.

Healing meant forgiveness, it meant coming home to myself after accepting that I was enough.

It's all fun and games until you start asking questions, until you start naming feelings. Because then it's too much to handle and we become guarded with cut-off defenses.

From pain comes creation. A defense mechanism projected through the healthy act of sublimation. What are your desires? Your impulses? And are they not socially accepted? Pour them into your craft, let the others gaze.

A longing for connection while acknowledging your own separateness is a step towards establishing individuation.

For someone who tends to romanticize, I appear to be quite the pessimist. I am a walking paradox – composed of clashing beliefs. I often wonder how many people exist within me.

I do not understand how I have gone through all this hurt, yet I am still full of love.

Indecision will be the death of me – where to eat for breakfast, what to wear to the gala, who to spend the rest of my life with.

Happiness, as well as a lack thereof, is reflected in the way you treat others.

I often wonder what kind of havoc would reign if we were to be driven solely by our animal instinct.

"Malignant," they said. Cruel and unkind and invasive. Always remember that you are stronger than what is happening to you. You are stronger than the intruder. This is surviving.

I miss who my mother was before the cancer invaded her body.

I am a sentimental being who has come to embrace not only my happiest moments but those in which I am suffering.

I've been living in the past and what I mean by that is that I haven't been living.

I was reminded of it suddenly but felt at ease when I realized that it doesn't bother me anymore. How I felt, whatever I felt, it's gone. Just like that. Because feelings are temporary. No matter how heavy the shame and embarrassment. It all fades.

There are people in this world who believe in a randomness, in accidents, in coincidences without reason. On the other end, there are people in this world who believe in an order, in meaning, in forming reasons to understand every bit of the human condition.

On behalf of tragedies, I find that people align themselves with the former belief. When it comes to romance, they envelop the latter.

I have a hard time believing that "everything happens for a reason." I'm more of a – we're all just casualties caught in the crossfire kind of believer.

There is a theory that proposes the notion of "no true-self."

I sat there, bewildered at the thought. For how many have loved or misunderstood or despised me, a rough draft. I then acknowledged that I will always be a rough draft, in constant transformation. We are never complete, in such a context that encompasses all the characteristics, beliefs, and experiences of an individual. Something will happen tomorrow and I won't be who I am today.

I often wonder if my ability to feel to such an extent is some form of punishment I've carried over from a past life. Because this pain does not belong to me and this sadness is not mine to bare and yet it weighs on me as if it were.

Every past relationship had the potential to be explored throughout my lifetime, regardless of why it ended. Looking back on memories of which I've shared with them – I have come to feel distant. I have come to feel as though I am a third party observer, a mere witness looking in on memories that no longer belong to me, as if they belonged to someone else, a past life. It's caused me to think about how many lives I could have lived, what path so and so could have led me to, what opportunities would have arisen, who I'd become. There is an endless realm of possibilities and I am overwhelmed at the thought.

I have come to the conclusion that life is like a multiple choice exam and I keep second guessing myself.

Jealousy is a form of imprisonment. It's poisonous to the soul, for our love, to one's relationships.

Silence is loud when you're alone with your thoughts.

When something isn't good for the soul, you can feel it in your bones. Being more in tune to ourselves can help us understand who or what is leaving us physically, emotionally, or mentally exhausted. Once we gain control of this, of understanding where the negative energy stems from, we can steer ourselves in the right direction – moving from an unnatural state of stagnation to growth.

I was too afraid to say it out loud. Using words to describe these feelings, to give them form and structure, thinking them into existence.

I feel as though I am being pulled from every direction – to love or move on, to wait or rebuild elsewhere.

The outbursts, the anger, the upset
is all a manifestation of an internal conflict
we must learn to resolve.

But who else is there to blame
when I am trapped
in the hell
that I built for myself.

The writer in me loves the thrill of affairs, of impulse, of the pain that elicits creation. The child in me remains playful, curious, and kind. The daughter in me is obedient, humble, grateful. The dreamer in me craves more. The woman in me remains soft, empathic, understanding, and faithful but is no longer as timid. I spent years attempting to divorce myself from the other, attempting to define myself in a single sentence without accepting that I am all of this at once.

You cannot look at me
without acknowledging the similarity
between my mother's eyes
my aunt's wit
and my father's sense of humor.

My brother's charm, my brother's
gestures. I am who I am – partly
because of them.

.

04. A CONCEPT

Selfish: where is your heart if not with me?

ill-fated: how often have we chosen to stay for those who already knew they were going to leave?

Heartbreak: I have died a thousand times and lived to tell the story.

11:11: time related to the notion of synchronicity, the prompting of a wish, fingers crossed, eyes closed, hoping the universe delivers your wants to your front door.

Cruelty: entertaining my feelings for the sake of your ego. The only thing you love, is knowing I love you.

Women: the softest creatures with the strongest bite.

Temptation: a fight between desires, a challenge to your commitment. Which is more prominent? What does the heart want and who does your mouth water for?

A disconnect: the man I couldn't stop thinking about was not the same man who's hands I was holding.

A mystery: something in me is drawn to you, I have tried desperately to understand what that is.

Hesitation: reaching for new hands when romantic love has proven itself temporary.

Challenge: who do you want to be? Why haven't you become it?

Speaking things into existence: you and I will one day have the opportunity to experience this longing.

Time: a man made concept, yet I continuously feel its hand at my throat. Everything past is lost and I struggle to grasp onto anything with meaning.

I have learned to be still, to be present, to be here. I have learned to close every door behind me while simultaneously opening those ahead.

An apology: to my younger-self for associating my worth with a man's attention.

Goal: to envelop self-assurance and a love so pure that my glow inspires others to love themselves, too.

Note: tomorrow is another day, a fresh start. You don't have to feel this way anymore.

Vivid: my imagination allows me to enter other realms while remaining seated.

Exhausted: my body aches, come kiss it.

Infidelity: you rolled over in bed, called me by another name. I asked how long it's been going on – you sat up in shame.

Infidelity cont'd: I have not forgotten the name of the woman he chose for the night after I laid by his side for years.

Betrayal: was she worth what we lost?

Men: hold me close, ruin me later.

Conflict: wanting to share my world but
struggling to find someone who understands it.

Levels: there are so many facets to my personality that tomorrow I may read a poem of mine and feel as though it was written by someone else.

Dreams: to find meaning in the distortions.

Note-to-self: you can't protect everyone. Some people will choose to learn the hard way. Let them.

Relentless: meant creating a door when it seemed as though the others were bolted shut.

Humble: understanding that the greatest difference among people lies in opportunity – not a lack of ability.

ABOUT THE AUTHOR

N.M.Sanchez is a Cuban-American writer based in the Magic City. She received her B.A. in psychology and is currently attending a clinical psychology doctoral program. *Initial Meeting* is her debut collection of poetry.

AUTHOR NOTE: I would like to take this moment to say thank you, a million times, thank you. I am filled with absolute warmth and gratitude.

Made in the USA
San Bernardino, CA
23 July 2018